THE KRYPTON FACTOR QUIZ BOOK

What two letters are missing?

R P T O N

If a total of 2969 digits are required to number the pages of a book, how many pages are there?

If you pull both ends,
will it make a knot?

Which of the principal Channel Islands is furthest south, and has St Helier as its capital?

This is the Krypton Factor challenge. How do you measure up? Try it and see!

QUIZ BOOK

By 'The Krypton Factor' team

Compiled by Nick Turnbull

Cartoons by David Hughes

ARROW BOOKS

Arrow Books Limited
17–21 Conway Street, London W1P 6JD

An imprint of the Hutchinson Publishing Group

London Melbourne Sydney Auckland
Johannesburg and agencies throughout
the world

First published 1984
Reprinted 1984

Text © Granada Television 1984
Illustrations © David Hughes 1984
Film stills © Warner Brothers, Walt Disney Productions,
Columbia Pictures, United International Pictures, and
Thorn-EMI Limited

Set in Linotron Times by
Input Typesetting Ltd, London SW19 8DR

Made and printed in Great Britain
by The Guernsey Press Co. Ltd
Guernsey, C.I.

ISBN 0 09 934840 3

Contents

Acknowledgements

We would like to extend our thanks to the following people: Nic Crawley of Warner Brothers publicity, Brian Burton and Julie Williams of Walt Disney Productions, Barbara de Lord of Columbia Pictures publicity, Beverley Yew of Thorn/EMI, and Rosemary Goodfriend of United International Pictures. A very special thanks to Vanessa Beresford.

The Krypton Factor Quiz Book is divided into five programmes. Each programme is made up of the five tests of 'The Krypton Factor', and they are designed to become progressively more difficult.

When you've finished each test, check your answers with the correct ones at the back of the book, count up your total score, then mark it down on the scorecard on page 119.

If you wish to be assessed for the television programme, send the completed application form from the back of this book (or copy to avoid spoiling the book) to: The Krypton Factor, Granada Television, Manchester M60 9EA.

Warning: If you are in any doubt about your fitness and you do not take regular strenuous exercise, you should seek medical advice before embarking on Krypton tests. Neither Granada Television nor Arrow Books can accept responsibility for any harm resulting from the fitness exercises in this book.

Have fun with the book. You never know – we could be seeing you next year!

Introduction

So, how well do you respond to a challenge? Very
well, you think. Maybe this book will give you some
idea, and who knows, *you* might be next year's
superperson.

Mind you, after sitting in 'The Krypton Factor's'
Quiz Master's chair for seven years and for just over
one hundred shows, you'd think that by now I could
spot a superperson at a thousand yards. But I'm
afraid not; age, sex, profession – there's no clue there,
and even when you've lined up forty-eight likely
candidates at the start of a series, it's still anybody's
guess. The studio lights, the cameras, the audience
– to say nothing of that assault course and ten million
armchair critics – they all have their effect and it
takes a lot of nerve to cope.

Just thinking about that for a moment, I've seen
some novel methods employed by some contestants
to beat those pressures. I remember a bank official
who buried a bottle of champagne at the end of the
assault course to give himself added incentive to win
– and he did. There was an outright winner one year
who wouldn't go near the studio without a little teddy
bear given to him by his children, and there was the
housewife who insisted on being last out of the
dressing-room, last into the make-up chair and last
to take her seat in the studio. I won't spoil the story
by telling you where she came in her heat!

Anyway, right now it's your turn. Have a go at all the tests – they can be difficult but then they should be since they're devised by the splendid, slightly sadistic team who've been with us since we started way back in 1977. Enjoy the book, but above all be totally honest with yourself and the very best of luck!

GORDON BURNS

PHYSICAL ABILITY

The Physical Ability tests are set by Charles Burton, Transglobal explorer, sailor and scientist. He was a guest contestant on the Christmas 1982 'Krypton Factor'

To succeed, you need to be fit – not only physically, but also mentally. For instance, on the Transglobe Expedition we trained hard – and were, therefore, in good condition physically, but because of the extreme conditions of cold we were to endure during the crossings of the North and South Poles, and the long periods of isolation, we had to be more mentally prepared than most.

The determination to succeed was also part of our mental training, a chance to test ourselves against odds that were, at times, overwhelming. For me, 'The Krypton Factor' offers the same kind of challenge, which is why I was delighted to help compile this book.

The series of exercises I have set become progressively more difficult. Use your common sense, and if you feel it's too much for you, for goodness sake, stop! Allow yourself a 15-second break between exercises. Most can be done in the comfort of your own home, and need no complicated equipment.

Good luck!

MENTAL AGILITY

The Mental Agility tests
are set by Dr Peter
Taylor, Principal Clinical
Psychologist working in
Kidderminster Health
District

'The key to success in this round has always been to
keep a cool head. For the contestant who is easily
flustered, Mental Agility can be a nightmare –
particularly on the programme, when the contestants
are up against the clock. The problems in this book
are slightly different from those on the screen in that
you're not required to remember anything, but you'll
need to concentrate just as hard.

I enjoyed setting them – I hope you enjoy answering
them and, remember, keep a cool head.

INTELLIGENCE TESTS

The Intelligence Tests are set by Dr Gerald Wickham, Lecturer in Mathematics, Manchester University

I've always preferred to think of these problems as testing a special kind of intelligence. If you get the answer wrong, it doesn't mean that you're unintelligent, only that you weren't sufficiently flexible in your thinking. Look for the 'unusual' way into the problem, think before you put pen to paper. As with the Intelligence Tests on the programme, the successful contestant is usually the one who first stands back and looks at the problem before tackling it. If all this proves anything, it's only that problem solving is a skill as opposed to a simple process of trial and error.

OBSERVATION TESTS

The Observation Tests
are set by Tony Dalton,
formerly a Lecturer with
the British Film Institute,
now a Senior Film
Researcher with
Granada Television

The film section of television's toughest quiz is always
a challenge to the contestants, but behind the scenes
it's a lot of fun, particularly for myself as I follow the
yearly search for current film clips. It's not easy to
find clips to suit our peculiar needs. Not only must
they fit the observation and information tests, but
they must also look good, be entertaining and give
enjoyment to contestants and viewers alike. Lastly,
the films must be British, or have been partially filmed
in Britain, so that we can easily locate and use one
of the extras. Success in finding these clips and
overcoming the problems involved is thanks to the
co-operation and immense help given to us by the
British film industry. This section in both the show
and the book would not have been possible without
their invaluable assistance. It is, therefore, to them
that I dedicate these pages.

Good luck with the quiz.

GENERAL KNOWLEDGE

The General Knowledge Tests are set by David Elias, Senior Lecturer in English at Trent Polytechnic, Nottingham

When you sit down to answer the 5 sets of General Knowledge questions in this book, remember you're the lucky ones. You've got time on your side. Not a lot, perhaps, but more time than our contestants who usually have to answer up to ten questions a minute, having to respond almost instantaneously under the pressure of competition. That's tough and who knows? Maybe you'll find out for yourself one day.

Krypton Factor General Knowledge questions are written so that the answer to one becomes part of the following question. *It is essential* that you ask someone to read the questions out to you; that person should allow you exactly 15 seconds a question.

Have fun with the questions in this book and don't forget – the next best thing to a good answer is a good guess!

Programme 1

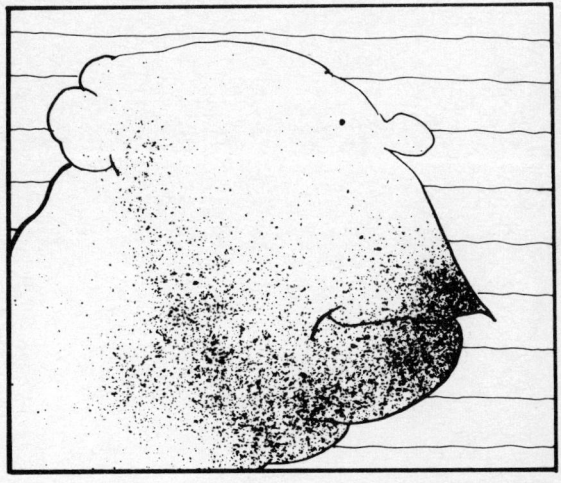

TEST 1: PHYSICAL ABILITY

Read warning on page 7.

Each of the following 4 exercises should be timed over 1 minute. The number of repetitions you can manage will give you your score.

1. Push-ups

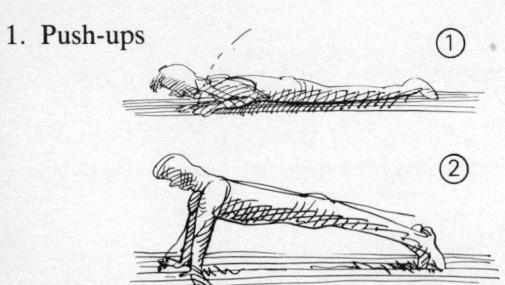

Repetitions:	15	14	13	12	
Score:	10	6	4	2	

2. Sit-ups

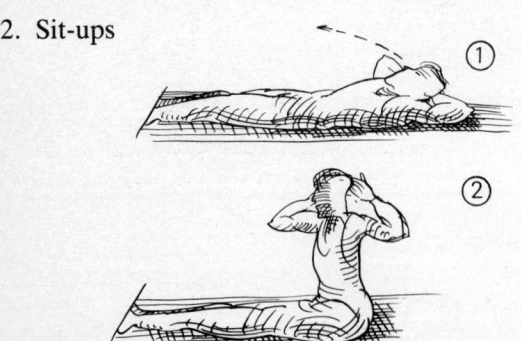

Repetitions:	15	14	13	12	
Score:	10	6	4	2	

3. Toe touching

Repetitions:	30	28	26	24
Score:	10	6	4	2

4. Squat jumps

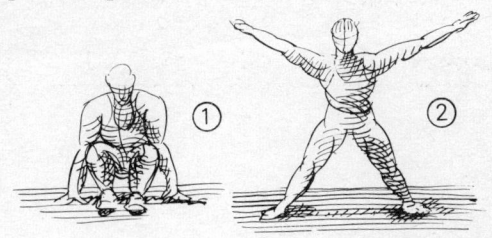

Repetitions:	25	22	20	17
Score:	10	6	4	2

5. Run one mile

Time in minutes:	10	11	12	13
Score:	10	6	4	2

TOTAL SCORE

TEST 2: MENTAL AGILITY

Score 2 points for each correct answer.
Target time is 20 minutes.

1. What two letters are missing?

    R P T O N

2. If **JFVHGRLMH** means questions,
   what does **KFAAOVH** mean?

3. Will these pieces make a Greek cross?

4. If Giles's father is Percy's son, what
   relation is Giles's son to Percy?

5.

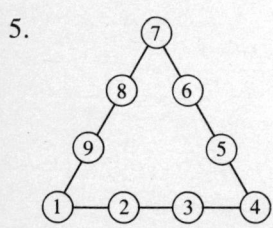

    Arrange the numbers 1 – 9 so that each
    side has the same total.

6. What's next in this
   series?   st nd rd th

7. What's next in this
   series?   A Z C X E

8.   1 2 5   2 6 20
                  is to
        4 3 6   8 9 24

   as   3 5 4   ? ? ? 6 15 16
                  is to
        6 8 7   ? ? ? 12 24 28

9.

   If you pull both ends, will it make a knot?

10. In a 10 storey block of flats, which floor
    is above the floor below the floor, below
    the floor above the floor above the floor,
    below the floor above the 5th?

                              TOTAL SCORE

−5

TEST 3: INTELLIGENCE

For each of these questions correctly answered, score 4 points.
Target time is 30 minutes.

1. If 129 players enter a knockout tennis tournament how many matches must be played?

2. These two squares placed side by side may be cut along the dotted lines to form a 5-piece jigsaw. How far should B be from A so that the 5 pieces may be reassembled to form a single square?

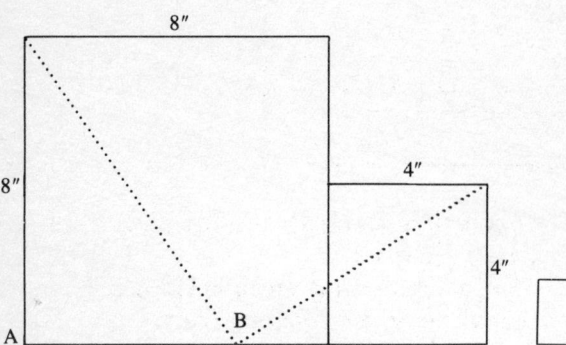

3. Place 4 black counters and 4 white counters alternately in a line. By making only 4 moves, each of a pair of 2 adjacent counters, and without altering the relative position of the pair, transform the line into a row of 4 black counters followed by 4 white counters.

4. A magic square is a square array of numbers which have the property that every row and column and each diagonal line have an equal sum. In this magic square, made up of all the numbers from 1 to 36 inclusive, fill in the missing squares.

	26	13	12	23	
	15	20	21	18	
	19	16	17	22	
	14	25	24	11	

5. 1. Only 5 horses finished the Krypton Grand National.
   2. The jockey wearing green finished just behind the jockey wearing ivory.
   3. The English jockey wore red.
   4. The Japanese jockey rode a 9-year-old.
   5. The Irishman had a glass of whiskey after the race.
   6. The American's horse was trained by Bert.
   7. The jockey who finished 3rd drank tea after the race.

8. The jockey wearing green drank coffee after the race.
9. The Frenchman wore yellow and he rode the winner.
10. The jockey who rode the horse trained by Mick drank milk after the race.
11. Fred trained the horse whose jockey wore yellow.
12. Shaun trained the 7-year-old.
13. It was a photo finish and in the photograph:

i) the horse ridden by the Frenchman was *next* to the horse ridden by the jockey wearing blue.

  ii) the horse trained by Joe was *next* to the 12-year-old.

  iii) the horse trained by Fred was *next* to the 10-year-old.

Questions:

a) Who were the trainers of the 1st/2nd/3rd/4th and last horse?

b) What is the nationality of the 1st/2nd/3rd/4th and last jockey?

c) Did the jockey riding the eleven-year-old drink coffee or champagne after the race?

TOTAL SCORE

TEST 4: OBSERVATION

Study the following pictures and their captions carefully. Then turn the page and answer the 10 questions. You have a maximum of 5 minutes. Score 2 points for each correct answer.

Stills from the film 'Never Say Never Again' reproduced by kind permission of Warner Brothers.

James Bond, or 007 as he is also known, is the world's most famous secret service agent and is licensed to kill. After 6½ weeks of intensive training and mock-combat, Bond is considered by the new M to be out of date, and he decides to scrap the famous double-0's of his agent. He sends Bond to Shrublands, a health clinic, for 2 weeks of diet and exercise.

In a conference room, senior NATO officers watch as an image of Ernst Stavro Blofeld, SPECTRE's leader and Bond's mortal enemy, flickers on to a screen. They listen whilst he tells them that he has hijacked 2 nuclear cruise missiles and that catastrophe can only be avoided by donating a payment, amounting to 25 per cent of their individual oil purchases.

Left: Maximilian Largo, agent Number 1 for SPECTRE, has masterminded the plans and it is he who hides the missiles at a location known only to him.

Below: After Blofeld's announcement to NATO, Largo pilots a helicopter to his magnificent private yacht called *The Flying Saucer*, a travelling home and operational base for Largo and his villains. The yacht is a mass of complicated electronic communications, capable of fantastic feats. Largo lives aboard the yacht with his mistress, Domino, the sister of Jack Patachi, a US Air Force officer.

Meanwhile, Bond is assigned by M, against M's better judgement, to go in search of Blofeld, Largo and the cruise missiles. He follows Largo to Nice and invites himself to a charity gala Largo is giving at a casino. There he meets Domino, and whilst he dances with her he tells her that her brother has been killed, according to Largo's instructions.

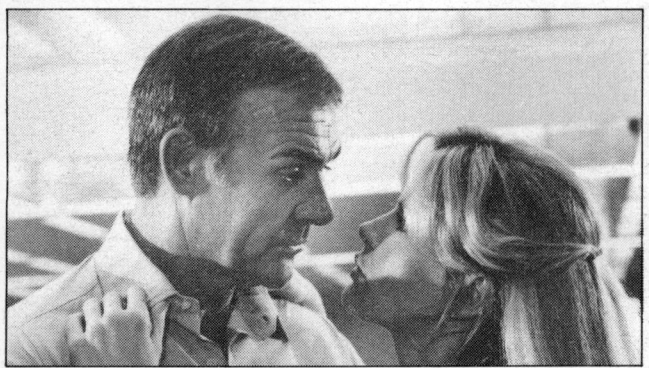

He returns to Largo's yacht and there finds Domino, who agrees to help him in his search for Largo and the bombs. Domino tells him where one of the bombs is hidden, it is right under the President's feet in Washington DC. However, she does not know where the second bomb is stowed away.

Following a hunch, Bond tracks down Largo in a special submarine, to a hidden bay. There they find a secret underground tunnel, but time is running short and only minutes now remain before SPECTRE will detonate the bomb.

The tunnel leads to a huge cave full of stalactites and stalagmites, and a 30-foot statue of a forgotten god. There, as the minutes tick by, Bond, Felix and Domino do battle with SPECTRE and Largo. Will Bond be in time, can he save the world from the holocaust. . . ?

The Krypton Factor

What you saw

1. What did Blofeld have in his breast pocket? *KERCHIEF*

2. What kind of pattern was on the dance floor, where Domino and Bond were dancing?

3. What did Largo have around his neck? *NECK TIE*

4. In the submarine, what was Bond leaning against? *BULK HEAD)*

5. How many decks above water did Largo's yacht have? *3*

What you read

1. How long was Bond on an intensive training course? *6½ WKS*

2. What did Blofeld demand as payment? *25%*

3. Apart from stalagmites and stalactites in the cave, what else was there? *STATUE*

4. What was the name of Largo's yacht? *FLYING SAUCER*

5. Where was the first bomb hidden? *WASHINGTON DC*

TOTAL SCORE

TEST 5: GENERAL KNOWLEDGE

Important: read Introduction on page 15 first.
This test should be completed in 5 minutes.
Score 1 point for each correct answer.

1. How often does a quinquennial event take place?

2. Which novelist wrote about the Five Towns in books like *Clayhanger* and *The Old Wives' Tale*?

3. Benedictine is a liqueur made by flavouring which spirit with herbs?

4. In which film of 1972 did Marlon Brando win an Oscar for his performance as Don Vito Corleone?

5. Who was the father of the gods in Roman mythology?

6. In which Italian city is Juventus football club based?

7. Which English king began the building of the White Tower of the Tower of London in 1078?

8. Which team won Rugby's Triple Crown in 1982, and were joint champions with France in 1983?

9. What name is given to the stretch of water separating Ireland from Scotland?

10. Which of the principal Channel Islands is furthest south, and has St Helier as its capital?

11. In which sport is a yellow jersey traditionally worn by the race leader?

12. What is obtained from chicle, the milky juice of a tropical American tree?

13. Chico, Gummo, Zeppo, Harpo and Groucho were known as what?

14. What was the real name of Mark Twain, the author of *Tom Sawyer*?

15. In which year did Clement Atlee become prime minister at the end of the Second World War?

16. Which prince led the 'Forty-Five' rebellion against George II in 1745?

17. Who played the title role of Bonnie in the 1967 film where Warren Beatty played Clyde?

18. Dundee, Eccles, Madeira and Genoa all gave their names to a kind of what?

19. The initials KKK denote which racist American organization?

20. Over what distance did Sebastian Coe win his Olympic gold medal in Moscow?

TOTAL SCORE

Programme 2

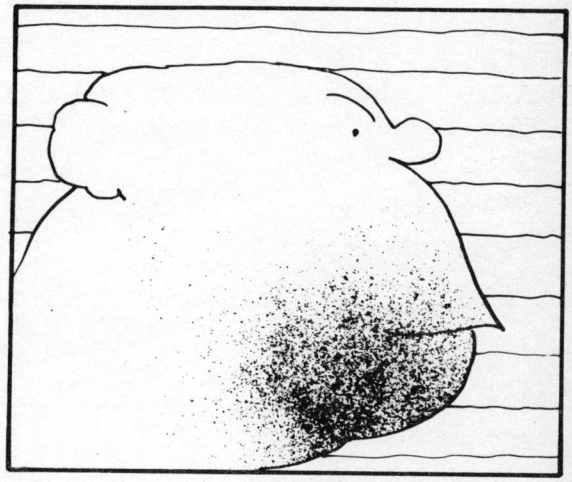

TEST 1: PHYSICAL ABILITY

Read warning on page 7.
Each of the following 4 exercises should be timed over
1 minute. The number of repetitions you can manage
will give you your score.

1. Push-ups

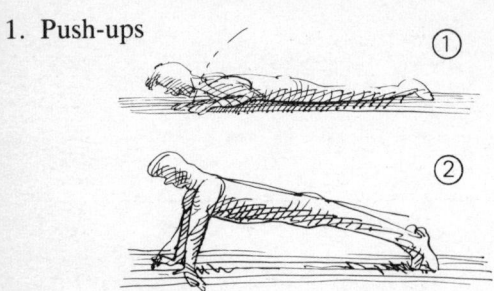

Repetitions:	20	19	18	17	
Score:	10	6	4	2	

2. Sit-ups

Repetitions:	20	19	18	17	
Score:	10	6	4	2	

3. Squat
   thrusts

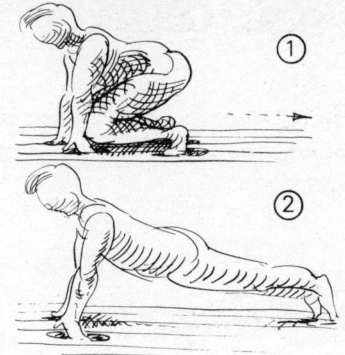

Repetitions:	35	32	29	27
Score:	10	6	4	2

4. Step-ups

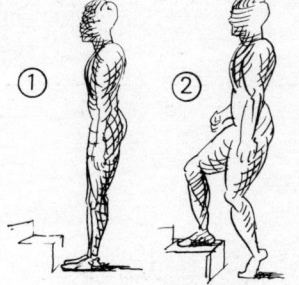

Repetitions:	40	38	36	34
Score:	10	6	4	2

5. Run one mile

Time in minutes:	7	8	9	10
Score:	10	6	4	2

TOTAL SCORE

TEST 2: MENTAL AGILITY

Score 2 points for each correct answer.
Target time is 20 minutes.

1. Which letter is
   missing?   M T W T F S

2. Divide these 2 crosses, using only 2
   straight lines so that the pieces can be
   re-arranged into a square.

3. If S h c E M d means riddle, what does
   D Z o g F q mean?

4. If you pull the ends will it make a knot?

5. Which letter comes before the letter,
   before the letter, after the letter, before
   the letter, after the letter, that's after the
   letter, before the letter after M in the
   alphabet?

6.   20 1 7   is to   3

   and

         14 4 6   is to   3

   as   8 7 3   is to   ?

7. What's next in this
   series?   ½ 1 2 5 10 20

8. What's next in this
   series?   2 3 6 18 108

9.

Three cards are face down in a row.
There is a king on the left of a king.
There is a spade on the left of a
diamond.
There is a king on the right of an ace.
There is a spade on the right of a spade.
Which card is which?

10.

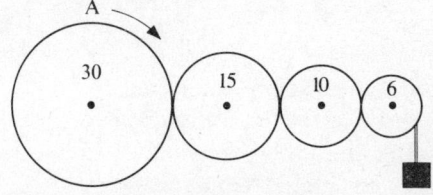

For every rotation clockwise of cog A,
how many rotations will the smallest cog
make?
Will the weight rise or fall?

TOTAL SCORE

TEST 3: INTELLIGENCE

For each of these questions correctly answered, score 4 points.
Target time is 30 minutes.

1. If a total of 2969 digits are required to number the pages of a book, how many pages are there?

2. Here are 12 shapes. They may be assembled to form an 8 × 8 square. How?

3. The following 7 letters when rearranged spell the word KRYPTON. Rearrangements may be performed only by removing the middle letter and replacing it at either end. Your task is to perform successive rearrangements according to this rule until the word KRYPTON appears.

K N Y T P R O

4. Complete this 6 × 6 magic square:

35	1	6	26	19	24
3	32	7	21	23	25
31	9	2	22	27	20
8	28	33			
30	5	34			
4	36	29			

5. A bag contains 12 billiard balls all the same colour, size and weight except one which is slightly heavier. How, in just 3 weighings, is it possible for you to single out the odd one using a balance?

TOTAL SCORE

TEST 4: OBSERVATION

Study the following pictures and their captions
carefully. Then turn the page and answer the 10
questions. You have a maximum of 5 minutes. Score
2 points for each correct answer.

Stills taken from 'The Jungle Book' by kind
permission of Walt Disney Productions.

Deep in the jungle a boy called Mowgli had been raised by a pair
of wolves and has never known man nor seen the man-village.
However, when the boy is 10 years of age, it is learned that Shere
Khan, the tiger, is returning to the hunting ground of the wolves
in search of man. This means that Mowgli is in danger and
Bagheera, the black panther, volunteers to return Mowgli to the
man-village, but Bagheera tells Mowgli that they will have to travel
through mysterious places, such as the Black Swamp, the trees of
snakes and a ruined city.

They set off through the jungle to find the village, in the direction
of the setting sun. Along the way Mowgli gets separated from
Bagheera and he gets caught up with Kaa, the python, who smacks
his lips and sets about hypnotizing the boy so that he can have
him for lunch. His attempts are thwarted by Bagheera and Mowgli
who successfully manage to tie Kaa up in knots.

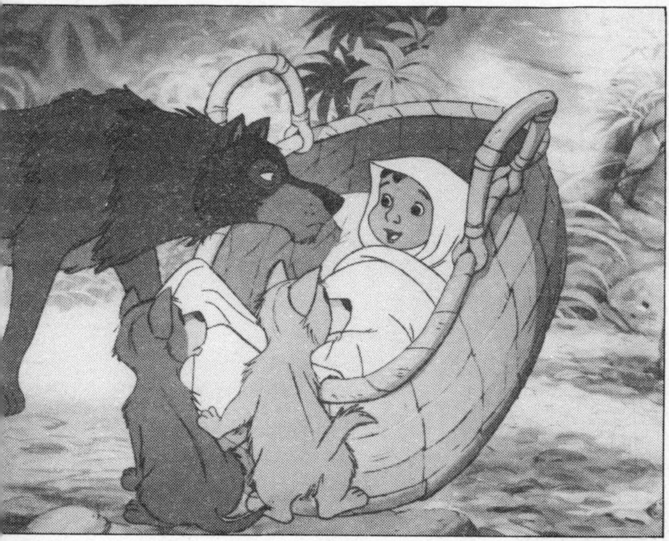

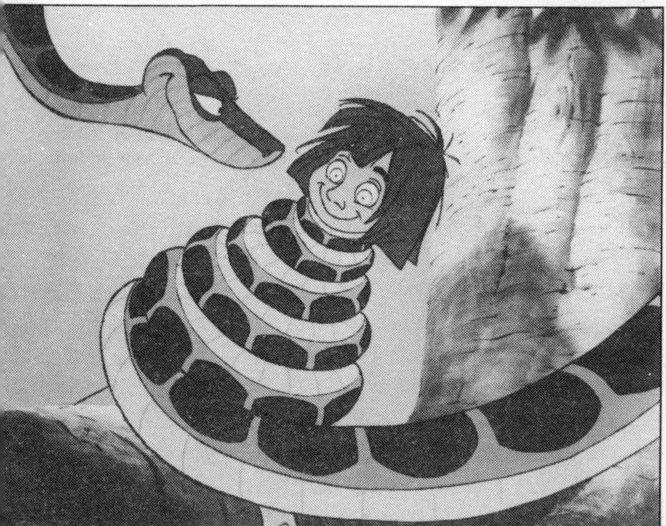

Fortunately, Mowgli manages to escape and next morning he and Bagheera are awakened by the sound of Colonel Hathi, leader of the elephant herd. Bagheera tells Mowgli of Colonel Hathi and the dawn patrol.

Later Mowgli's high-spirited antics exasperate Bagheera into temporarily deserting the boy who is immediately befriended by Baloo, the bear, who sings his own philosophy to Mowgli. The two of them, watched by Bagheera, float off down the river, and Baloo tells Mowgli that he would make 'one swell bear'.

Almost immediately Mowgli is kidnapped by a band of monkeys who carry him off to the ruins of a temple.

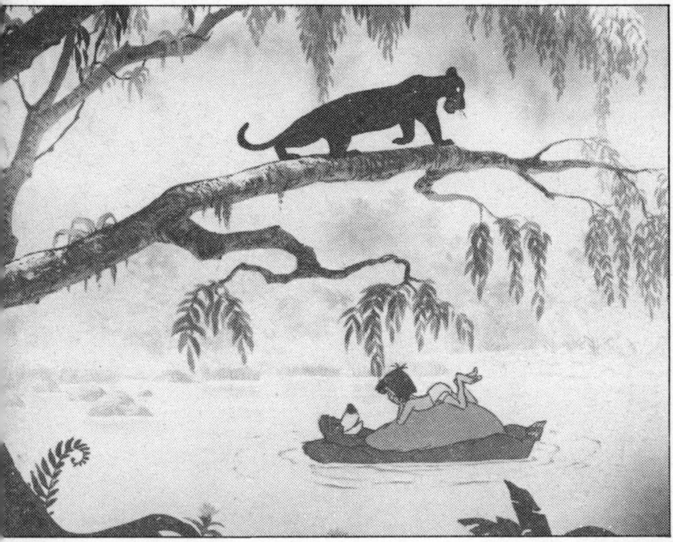

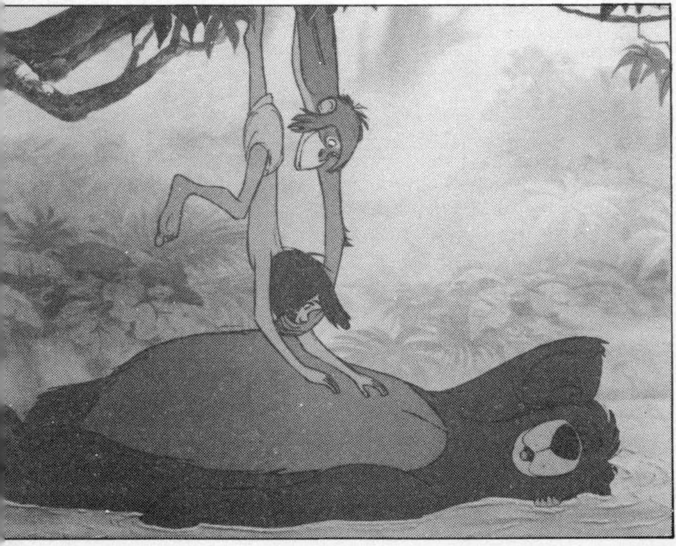

In the temple, Mowgli is eagerly welcomed by King Louis, the ape-king, who suffers from delusions of grandeur and imagines himself as already almost human. He promises to allow the jungle boy to remain with him in exchange for man's 'secret of the red flower' – fire!

Meanwhile, Bagheera and Baloo arrive on the scene and Baloo, disguised as a glamorous female ape, tries to impress King Louis with his own peculiar type of dancing.

After the 3 adventurers escape, Mowgli finds out that Bagheera has convinced Baloo that he must be returned to the man-village for his own safety and they make their way through the jungle, away from Shere Khan, who is now in pursuit.

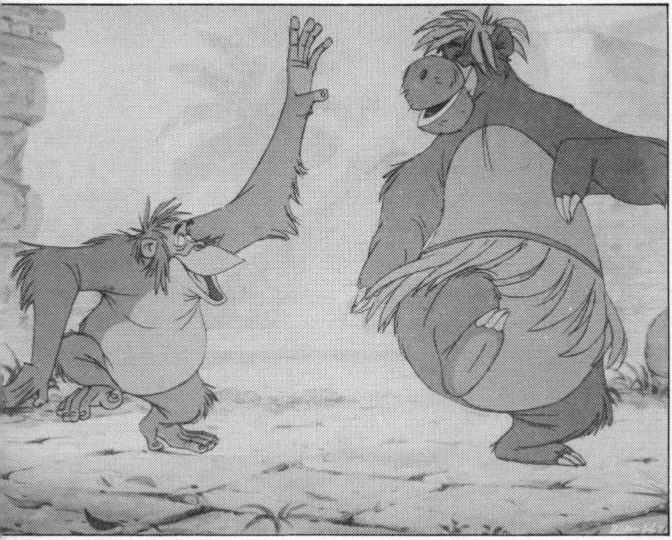

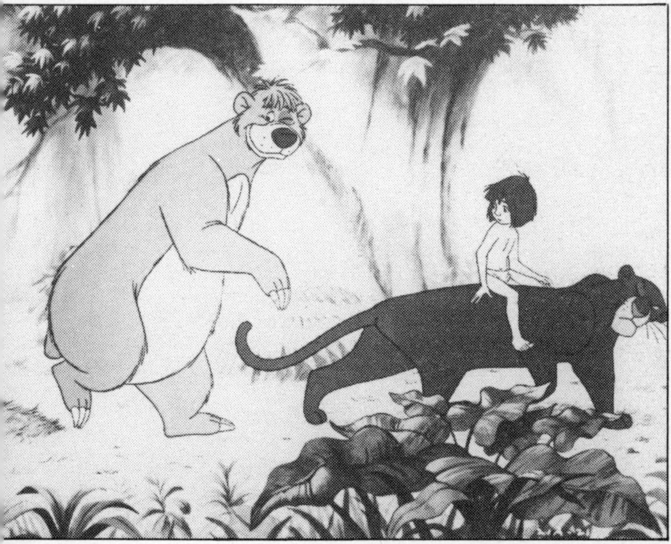

What you saw

1. How many wolf-cub puppies were seen looking into the baby Mowgli's basket?

2. How many elephants in Colonel Hathi's parade had tusks, excluding Colonel Hathi himself?

3. What did Mowgli have on his head when talking to King Louis in the ruined temple?

4. What did Baloo use for a mouth to imitate the monkeys when he was dancing with King Louis?

5. On whose back was Mowgli riding when the 3 adventurers made their escape from King Louis?

What you read

1. How old was Mowgli when he left the wolves?

2. In which direction did Bagheera take Mowgli to find the man-village?

3. What did King Louis want from Mowgli?

4. What was the name of Colonel Hathi's elephant parade?

5. Name two of the places Bagheera told Mowgli they would have to travel through to reach the man-village.

TOTAL SCORE

TEST 5: GENERAL KNOWLEDGE

Important: read Introduction on page 15 first.
This test should be completed in 5 minutes.
Score 1 point for each correct answer.

1. In which city was the late Shah of Iran buried in 1980?

2. Which mammals of the order *Chiroptera* have varieties called horseshoe, fruit and vampire?

3. Who replaced the dictator Batista in 1959 as ruler of Cuba?

4. Which of horse racing's 5 classics is run at Doncaster over 1¾ miles each autumn?

5. What was the name of the legendary sword pulled out of a stone by King Arthur?

6. In which of Shakespeare's plays do the characters Caliban and Ariel appear?

7. Which sport has classes called Tornado, 470, Soling and Flying Dutchman?

8. The Sailor King was the nickname of the ruler of Britain from 1830 to 1837. Who was he?

9. What name is given to a 4-sided figure with only one pair of sides parallel?

10. Which London street connects Piccadilly Circus and Oxford Circus?

11. Which regency novelist wrote *Mansfield Park*, *Persuasion* and *Emma*?

12. What special subject does an osteologist study?

13. To which island was Napoleon Bonaparte exiled in 1814?

14. Albany is the capital of the state of the USA called the 'Empire State'. Which is that?

15. Which Yorkshire football club is nicknamed 'The Owls' and plays at Hillsborough?

16. In which sport are competitions held for the Sheffield Shield, the Plunket Shield and the Ranji Trophy?

17. In Britain it's called a bowler hat. What do Americans call it?

18. Which country is divided by a stretch of water called the Dardanelles?

19. Traditionally turkey is eaten in the USA on the last Thursday of November. What is that holiday called?

TOTAL SCORE

The Krypton Factor

Programme 3

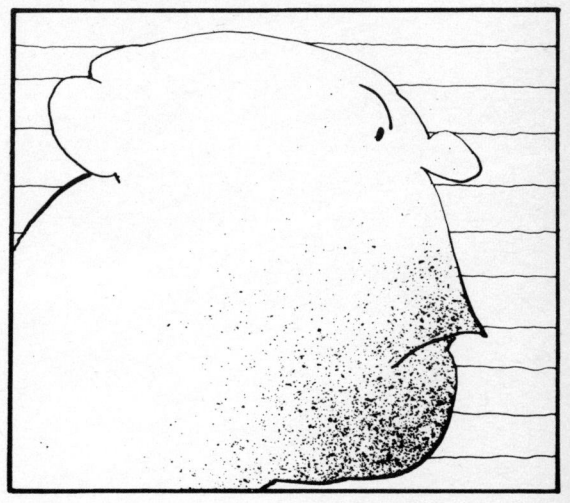

TEST 1: PHYSICAL ABILITY

Read warning on page 7.
Each of the following 4 exercises should be timed over 1 minute. The number of repetitions you can manage will give you your score.

1. Push-ups

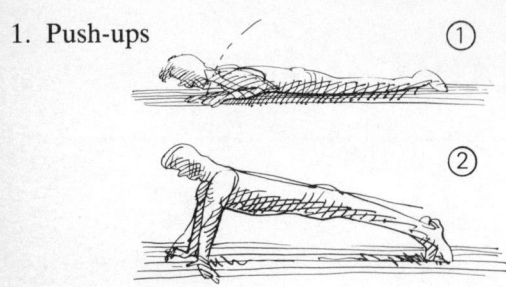

Repetitions:	25	22	21	20	
Score:	10	6	4	2	

2. Sit-ups

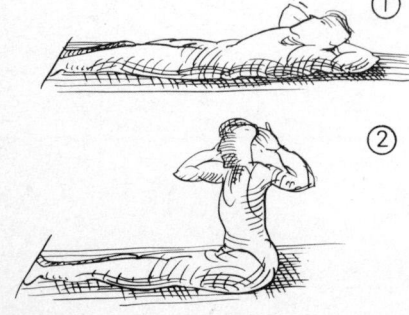

Repetitions:	25	22	21	20	
Score:	10	6	4	2	

3. Squat thrusts

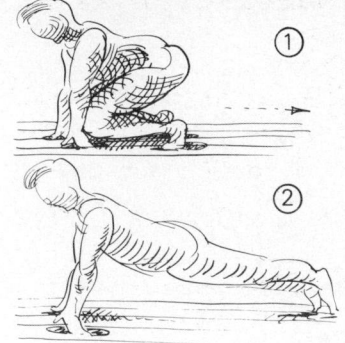

Repetitions:	40	38	36	34
Score:	10	6	4	2

4. Toe touching

Repetitions:	40	36	34	32
Score:	10	6	4	2

5. Run one mile

Time in minutes:	9	10	11	12
Score:	10	6	4	2

TOTAL SCORE

——The Krypton Factor——

TEST 2: MENTAL AGILITY

Score 2 points for each correct answer.
Target time is 20 minutes.

1. What two are missing from this set?

   9 8 A 3 6 Q 1 5 2 K 4 7

2. Divide this cross with
   four straight lines so
   that the five pieces
   can be re-arranged
   to make a square.

3. If 1 13 7 9 14 5 means enigma, what
   does 5 22 12 15 19 5 18 mean?

4. If you pull both ends,
   will it make a knot?

5. A B C D E
   F G H I J
   K L M N O
   P Q R S T
   U V W X Y

Which letter is on the right of the letter above
the letter to the right of the letter above the
letter to the left of the letter above the X?

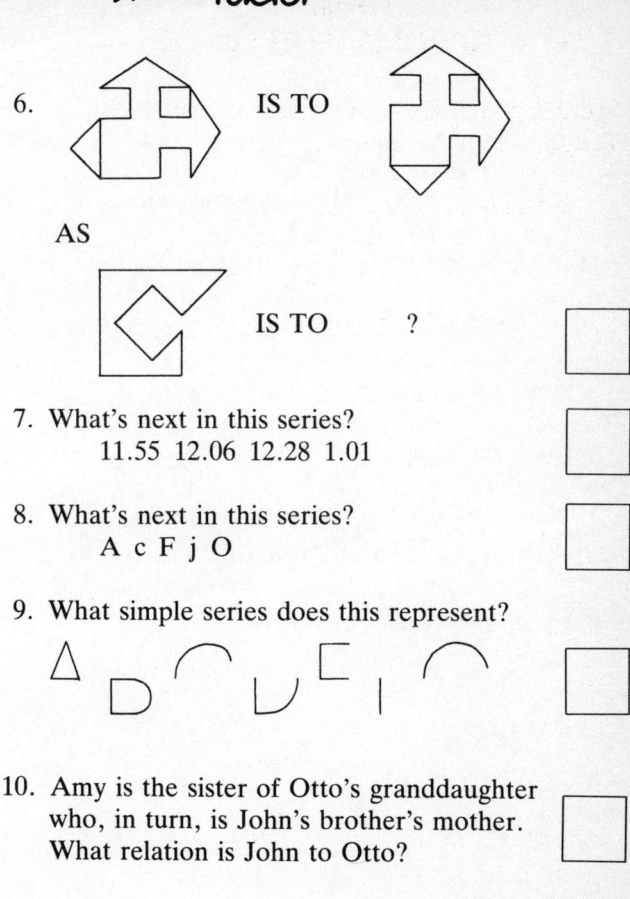

6.   IS TO

AS

        IS TO   ?

7. What's next in this series?
   11.55 12.06 12.28 1.01

8. What's next in this series?
   A c F j O

9. What simple series does this represent?

10. Amy is the sister of Otto's granddaughter
    who, in turn, is John's brother's mother.
    What relation is John to Otto?

TOTAL SCORE

TEST 3: INTELLIGENCE

For each of these questions correctly answered, score 4 points.
Target time is 30 minutes.

1. A party of 6 men wish to explore an uncharted desert. Assuming that each man can walk on average 30 miles per day carrying enough provisions to last him 4 days and given that the party may establish depots en route, find the maximum distance into the desert that one of the party may penetrate.

2. The following figure may be cut along 4 straight lines so that the resulting 5 pieces may be reassembled to form a square. How do you do it?

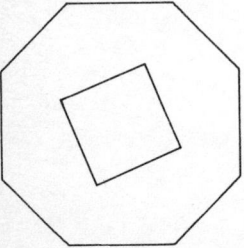

3. In this problem involving 3 black counters and 3 white counters placed on 7 squares in a row, your task is to exchange the locations of the black and white pieces. The black counters may only move from right to left. If the square next to a piece

is occupied by a piece of the opposite colour and the square beyond that is unoccupied then it can leap over that piece on to that unoccupied square.

4. There are 5 missing numbers including the number 3 which are all less than 50 and which make this square magic. Find the remaining 4 and place them in their correct position.

	71	5	23
53		37	1
17	13		31
	7	19	

5.   SEND
    + MORE
    = MONEY

Given that each letter corresponds to a unique digit, what do the letters in the above sum represent?

TOTAL SCORE

TEST 4: OBSERVATION

Study the following pictures and their captions carefully. Then turn the page and answer the 10 questions. You have a maximum of 5 minutes. Score 2 points for each correct answer.

Stills from the film 'Krull' by kind permission of Columbia Pictures.

Somewhere beyond our universe there is a distant world. A world where twin suns rise, good triumphs over evil and love prevails: a world called 'Krull'. On a planet that is not our planet, at a time that is not our time, The Beast with his hideous slayers is closing in on the White Castle where the Princess Lyssa is to marry Prince Colwyn.

At the climax of the ceremony, the slayers attack the castle and Princess Lyssa is captured and carried away to The Beast's Black Fortress.

Prince Colwyn must now seek out the Black Fortress, and sets out on his quest to recover his bride. On the way, he recovers the secret Glaive, the repository of all the power for good on Krull, by plunging his hand into boiling lava and remaining unscathed.

Left: With the magic Glaive, Colwyn's quest begins in earnest, and along the way he encounters the fiercely loyal Torquil who is the leader of a band of 7 cut-throats, all of whom are willing to travel at his side although each knows it could mean death.

Having once enlisted the robbers to his cause, Colwyn offers to unlock their gyves. However, Torquil swears they will continue to wear them until their task is successfully completed.

The Ancient Widow of the Web sits at the centre of the crystal spider's cocoon and she is willing to give the gift of her knowledge and so help Colwyn in return for the ultimate sacrifice of the death of one of his band.

Above: Attaining the Widow's lair, Ynyr brings youth back to the woman he once loved so that she will tell him the location of The Beast's Fortress. To escape with the information, he must carry the sands from her hour-glass in his hands, knowing that when they run away both he and the Widow will die.

Right: A slayer guards one of the living, moving tunnels of the Black Fortress. One of these tunnels leads to Princess Lyssa, and Colwyn, deep in the depths of the Fortress, has to confront her captor, a creature so terrible that no one has ever seen it and lived to tell the tale.

What you saw

1. In the second picture, what was Princess Lyssa wearing on her head?

2. How many points were there on the Glaive?

3. How many men in the first picture of the robbers were holding knives or swords?

4. In the fifth picture, what is the robber on the right sitting on?

5. What was the slayer guarding the fortress tunnels carrying?

What you read

1. What was unusual about the early morning on Krull?

2. Where were Colwyn and Lyssa to be married?

3. How many men were there in Torquil's band?

4. What did Ynyr have to carry from the widow's web?

5. What did Colwyn have to do to recover the Glaive?

TOTAL SCORE

TEST 5: GENERAL KNOWLEDGE

Important: read Introduction on page 15 first.
This test should be completed in 5 minutes.
Score 1 point for each correct answer.

1. Who succeeded Sir Alec Douglas-Home as prime minister in 1964?

2. By what name is John Thomas Wilson, former world professional darts champion, better known?

3. Which Irish dramatist wrote 'Riders to the Sea' and 'The Playboy of the Western World'?

4. The musical 'Song of Norway' is about the life of which composer?

5. Griffin, Samoyed and Borzoi are breeds of which animal?

6. In which sport do men compete annually for Doggett's Coat and Badge?

7. Caviar is obtained from the roe of which fish?

8. In 1967, who was the first surgeon to carry out a successful human heart transplant?

9. Great Horned, Tawny and Barn are varieties of which bird?

10. Who wrote the original stories about the 'Fat Owl of the Remove', Billy Bunter of Greyfriars School?

11. Who wrote and directed the comedy films 'Young Frankenstein', 'High Anxiety' and 'Blazing Saddles'?

12. On which river does Middlesbrough stand?

13. Motor cycling – what do the initials TT stand for in TT races?

14. In cricket, the NatWest Trophy replaced which previous one day competition in 1981?

15. How many gills are there in a pint?

16. The mouth of a river can be described by using the fourth letter of the Greek alphabet. What is it?

17. Which first division football team play at The Dell when at home?

18. Of which South American country is Bogota the capital?

19. Which birds make up the family *Columbidae*, including varieties called Ring, Stock and Turtle?

20. A dove was the second bird that Noah sent out from the ark. What was the first?

TOTAL SCORE

Programme 4

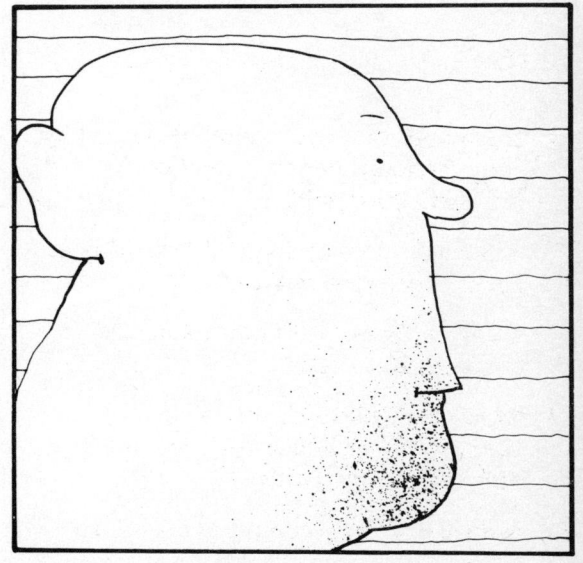

TEST 1: PHYSICAL ABILITY

Read warning on page 7.
Each of the following 4 exercises should be timed over
1 minute. The number of repetitions you can manage
will give you your score.

1. Push-ups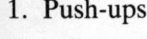

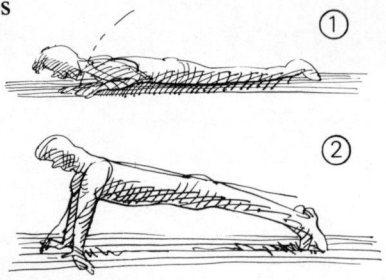

Repetitions:	27	25	23	22
Score:	10	6	4	2

2. Sit-ups

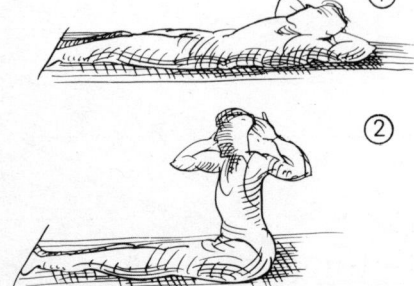

Repetitions:	27	25	23	22
Score:	10	6	4	2

3. Squat thrusts

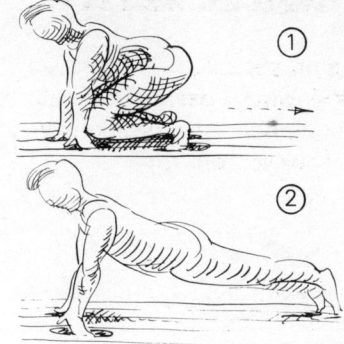

Repetitions:	50	45	40	38
Score:	10	6	4	2

4. Step-ups

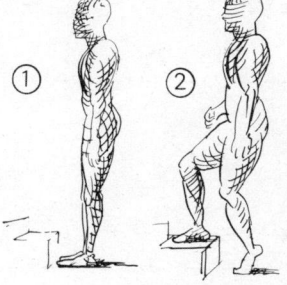

Repetitions:	50	45	40	38
Score:	10	6	4	2

5. Run one mile

Time in minutes:	6	7	8	9
Score:	10	6	4	2

TOTAL SCORE

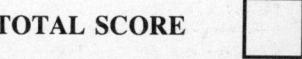

TEST 2: MENTAL AGILITY

Score 2 points for each correct answer.
Target time is 20 minutes.

1. What's missing from this
   sequence?   5 20 1 − 4 13

2. Divide this cross,
   using 2 straight lines
   so the pieces can be
   rearranged into a
   square.

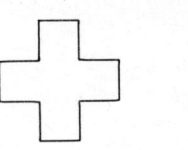

3. If   11 81 52 61 02 51 41   means krypton,
   what does   31 12 91 02   mean?

4.

   If you pull both ends, will it make a knot?

5. 1   2   3   4   5
    6   7   8   9   10
   11   12   13   14   15
   16   17   18   19   20
   21   22   23   24   25

   Which number is below the number that's
   twice the number to the left of the
   number that's half the number to the
   right of the number below the 8?

6. 12 2 10 9   is to   6 8 4 3

                as

   6 7 10 11   is to   ?

7. What's next in this series?   2.236 2.00 1.732 1.414

8. What's next in this series?   Y Y H L Y

9.

Which of the dice above cannot be made from this plan?

10.

Make only one change so that full and empty pints alternate.

TOTAL SCORE

TEST 3: INTELLIGENCE

For each of the questions correctly answered, score 4 points.
Target time is 30 minutes.

1. The number of my house is a 3-digit number. The number of my friend's house is the reverse of my number. The last digit in the difference between our 2 numbers is 3. What is the difference between our two numbers?

2. A room is 30 feet long, 12 feet wide and 12 feet high. On the middle line of one of the small side walls and 1 foot from the ceiling is a spider. On the middle line of the opposite wall and 11 feet from the ceiling is a fly. Assuming the fly is paralysed by fear and remains still, find the length of the shortest route along which the spider may crawl to his prey.

3. Four married couples have to cross a river by means of a boat which can be rowed by 1 person and will carry at most 3 passengers. What is the least number of passages from one bank to another in which the transfer may be effected, it being agreed that no woman is to be in the society of a man unless her husband is present!

4. By arranging the following dominoes in the frame provided construct 'a magic dominoes square' so that the sums of the dots in each row, column and diagonal are all equal.

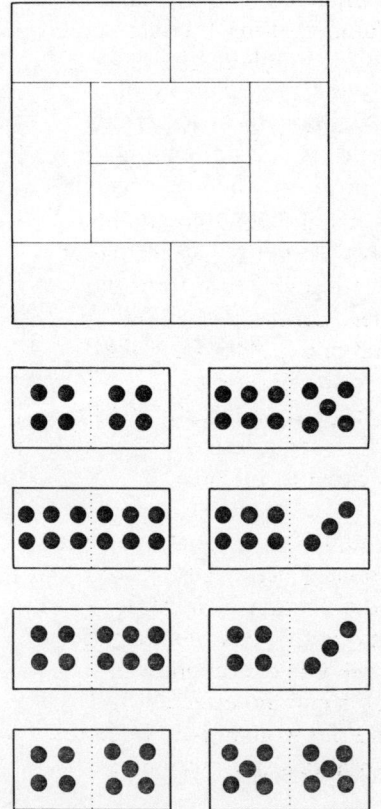

5. A professor of mathematics is out strolling with his friend who casually asks of the professor, 'Do you have any children?' 'Yes' he replies, 'I have three daughters.' 'How old are they?' asks the friend. 'Well,' says the professor, 'the product of their ages is 72.' 'That's not enough information,' retorts the friend. 'OK,' says the professor. 'How about this – the sum of their ages equals the number of your house.' A little thought prompts the friend to say that this is still not enough information. The professor then reveals all by stating that his eldest daughter plays the violin! What are his daughters' ages?

TOTAL SCORE

TEST 4: OBSERVATION

Study the following pictures and their captions carefully. Then turn the page and answer the 10 questions. You have a maximum of 5 minutes. Score 2 points for each correct answer.

Stills from the film 'Jaws 3-D' reproduced by kind permission of United International Pictures.

At Sea World in Florida, an ingenious new 'undersea kingdom' is about to open. Mike Brody is chief engineer for the project. A maze of transparent tunnels beneath the park's lagoon will take visitors to a world teeming with exotic undersea life. There's even an aquatic fun-house and a gourmet restaurant. Unknown to the people whose job it is to complete the sea kingdom for opening day, there is an unseen lurking menace about to cause chaos and terror.

Also working on the undersea project is Kathryn Morgan, a marine biologist. She has spent many years in bringing this futuristic park to fruition.

Both Mike and Kathryn have become very close, but unfortunately the completion of the undersea kingdom will have to signal the end of their love affair. Mike is moving to his next construction project in South America, and Kathryn has the chance of an appointment with the Scripps Marine Institute.

Attractions on the park include 'Treasures of the Spanish Main', a fake galleon loaded with pirate swag, and 'Poseidon's Wonders', a scenic marvel of make-believe coral reefs. Also there are fantastic displays of water-skiing and acrobatics, performed on the lake above the undersea kingdom.

Whilst all is still being prepared for the grand opening of the park, the last to arrive is the celebrated young sea photographer,

Philip FitzRoyce, whose flamboyance can turn even a casual greeting into a media event.

Kathryn and Mike take an instinctive dislike to FitzRoyce, but it is offset by the pleasure of welcoming Sean Brody, Mike's brother who has come to Sea World to share his big brother's triumph, and to continue his single-minded pursuit of the opposite sex, notably the park's water-skier, Kelly Ann Bokowski, and perhaps even challenge an obsessive fear of swimming, which dates back to his Amity childhood.

On the eve of the opening, Sea World officers are given

their last-minute instructions. On the surface all seems well. The press sip champagne in a hillside pavilion as water-skiers rehearse an intricate human pyramid. Behind the scenes, a lone diver descends to repair just one minor problem . . . a faulty sea gate through which a great white shark has entered the lagoon.

Back on dry land, Mike, Kathryn and Philip FitzRoyce frantically search for a method to destroy the terror. Mike remembers his boyhood encounter with other Great Whites, and tries to convince the others of the difficult task ahead.

What you saw

1. What was the emblem of Sea World?

2. What did Kathryn have round her neck in the portrait of her?

3. What shaped object was on the post which Mike was leaning against on the beach with Kathryn?

4. How many men were in the water-skiing pyramid?

5. In the portrait of Philip FitzRoyce, what time did his watch show?

What you read

1. In which part of the world was Mike's next project going to take place, after Sea World?

2. What were 'Poseidon's Wonders'?

3. Where were the press 'sipping champagne' on the opening day?

4. Where did Kathryn hope to get a job?

5. What was the name of Sean's girlfriend?

TOTAL SCORE

TEST 5: GENERAL KNOWLEDGE

Important: read Introduction on page 15 first.
This test should be completed in 15 minutes.
Score 1 point for each correct answer.

1. 'Chattanooga Choo-Choo' and
   'Moonlight Serenade' were made
   popular by which American band-leader
   and trombone player?

2. What kind of creatures are miller's
   thumb, alewife and pickerel?

3. Who wrote the operas 'Albert Herring',
   'Peter Grimes' and 'Billy Budd'?

4. In 1967, which football club were the first
   British winners of the European Cup?

5. Who suggested the theory of natural
   selection in 1859?

6. Dar-es-Salaam is the capital of which
   African country?

7. In Indian cookery, 'tandoori' means a
   dish is cooked in a tandoor. What is a
   tandoor?

8. Who was the wife of Louis XVI of
   France, nicknamed 'the baker', and
   executed with him in 1793?

9. Which heroine married Mr Rochester in Charlotte Brontë's novel of 1847 about a governess?

10. The city of Buenos Aires stands at the mouth of which river?

11. Which sport is played on an area including foul lines, home plate and a mound?

12. Where is the British naval base of Scapa Flow?

13. Which instrument of the orchestra has a name meaning literally 'pleasant sound' in Greek?

14. The English football club who won the 1981 UEFA cup play at home at Portman Road. Who are they?

15. For his part in which film did Henry Fonda win his only Oscar, shortly before he died in 1982?

16. What's the chemical symbol for silver?

17. With which sport do you associate the names of Giacomo Agostini, Kenny Roberts and Geoff Duke?

18. Who was the composer of the Ring Cycle and 'The Flying Dutchman'?

19. Variola is the name of a disease which the World Health Organization claims has now been completely eliminated. Which disease is it?

20. Who wrote the novels *Jo's Boys* and *Little Women*?

TOTAL SCORE

Programme 5

TEST 1: PHYSICAL ABILITY

Read warning on page 7.
Each of the following 4 exercises should be timed over 1 minute. The number of repetitions you can manage will give you your score.

1. Sit-ups

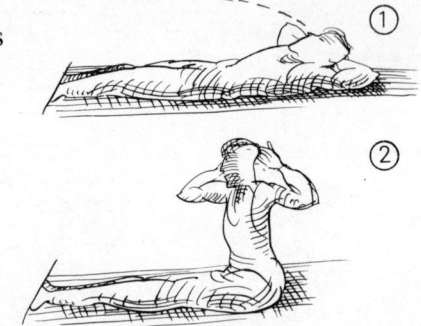

Repetitions:	30	27	25	23	
Score:	10	6	4	2	

2. Squat thrusts

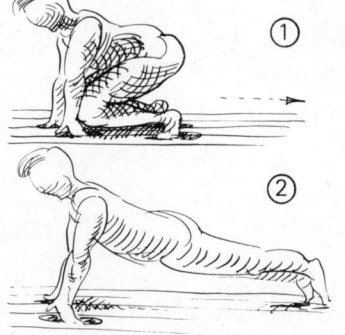

Repetitions:	60	55	50	45	
Score:	10	6	4	2	

3. One-arm
   push-ups

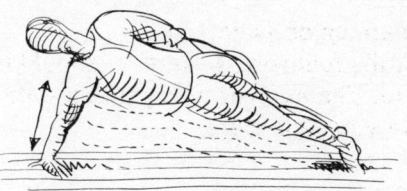

Repetitions:	10	8	6	5	
Score:	10	6	4	2	

4. Pull-ups

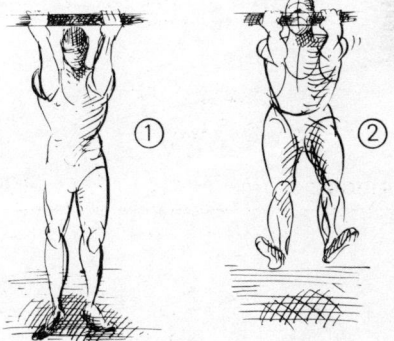

Repetitions:	20	19	18	17	
Score:	10	6	4	2	

5. Run one mile

Time in minutes:	5	6	7	8	
Score:	10	6	4	2	

TOTAL SCORE

TEST 2: MENTAL AGILITY

Score 2 points for each correct answer.
Target time is 20 minutes.

1. What's missing from this
   sequence?   R O Y G B I

2. Divide this cross with
   2 straight lines so
   the pieces can be
   rearranged into a
   square. (NB. Solution
   must be different
   from section 4.)

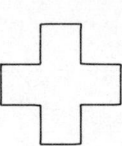

3. If T Q O V V L P P V means solutions
   what does Q T R C N H N U mean?

4.

   If you pull both ends, will it make a knot?

5. 1   2   3   4   5
    6   7   8   9 10
   11 12 13 14 15
   16 17 18 19 20
   21 22 23 24 25

What number is below the number that's twice the number that's below the number that's 1/3 of the number to the left of the number that's twice the number that's ¼ of the number to the right of 19?

6.

IS TO

AS

IS TO   ?

7. What's next in this series?   285 433 247

8. What's next in this series?   6.58 4.41 2.24 24.07

9. What word does this spell?

10. What is the minimum number of weights needed to weigh up to 40 ounces on an ordinary balance? What are the weights?

TOTAL SCORE

The Krypton Factor

TEST 3: INTELLIGENCE

For each of these questions correctly answered, score 4 points.
Target time is 30 minutes.

1. In the following long division all the digits except some of the 4's have been omitted. Fill in the missing digits; the answer is unique!

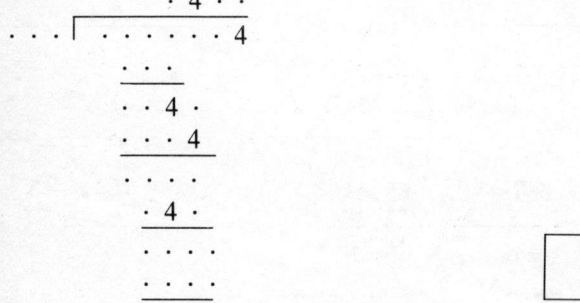

2. The following set of 24 triangular
   dominoes may be assembled according to
   the usual rules of dominoes to create a
   hexagon with 1's all round the edge. Can
   you do it?

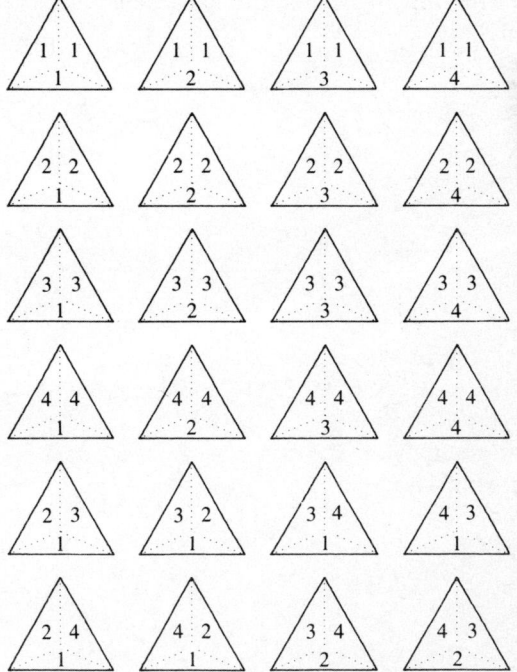

All the triangles are equal and have equal
sides.

3. The 'Great Northern Shunting Puzzle'

The diagram shows a railway line with 2 sidings connected at A. The portion of the rails at A which is common to the 2 sidings is long enough to permit a single wagon to run in or out of it but too short for the engine. Hence if the engine runs up a siding, it must return along the same route. The problem is to interchange the position of the 2 wagons.

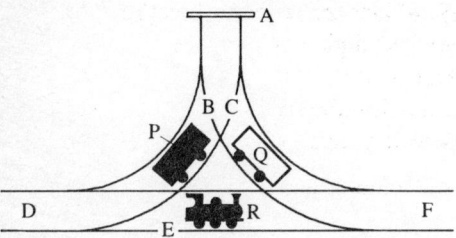

4. In this figure, the reader may place the numbers 2, 4, 5, 6, 9, 10, 11 and 13 at the 8 points of the inner star so that the sums of the numbers at the corners of every square in the figure are equal.

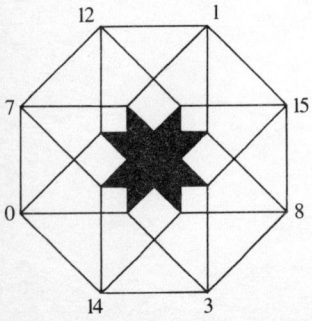

5. Jones wishes to find out what number
   house Smith lives in. He knows it to be
   between 13 and 1300, so he asks questions
   as follows:

Jones: Is it less than 500?
Smith: (answers but lies)
Jones: Is it a perfect square?
Smith: (answers but lies)
Jones: Is it a perfect cube?
Smith: (answers truthfully)
Jones: Now just tell me whether the
         second digit is a 1 or not.
Smith: (answers)
Jones: Your number is x.
Smith: No, it is not.

Can you say what it is?

TOTAL SCORE

TEST 4: OBSERVATION

Study the following pictures and their captions carefully. Then turn the page and answer the 10 questions. You have a maximum of 5 minutes. Score 2 points for each correct answer.

Stills from the film 'Kind Hearts and Coronets' by kind permission of Thorn-EMI Limited.

Louis Mazzini is the son of an English mother and an Italian father. His mother was the daughter of the 7th Duke of Chalfont, and when she eloped with her handsome singer, her only regret was the attitude of her family. She died of a broken heart several years after her husband's death, and it is because of his mother's treatment by her family that Louis sets out on a determined career of homicide. Brought up with a knowledge of his family history, Louis is always acutely conscious that it is theoretically possible for him to inherit the dukedom.

One by one, Louis must pick off the family heirs to attain the dukedom. The first to disappear in a series of cleverly conceived 'accidents' is Ascoyne D'Ascoyne, for whom Louis arranges an untimely death by causing him to go head-first over the weir in a punt.

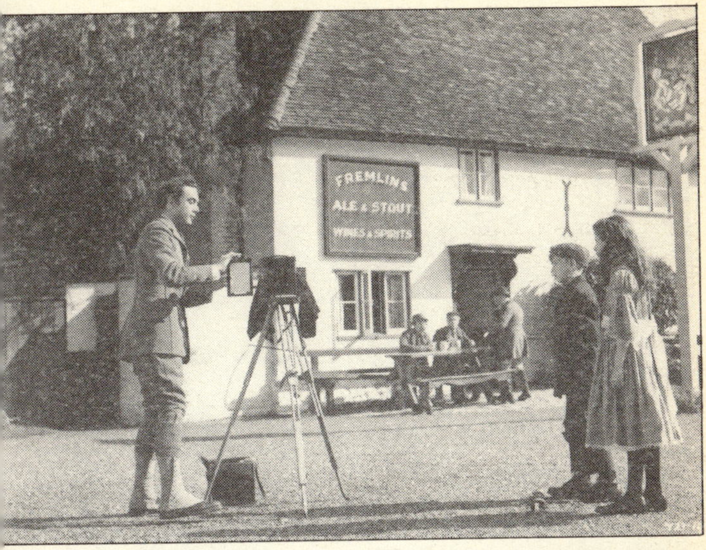
FREMLINS
ALE & STOUT
WINES & SPIRITS

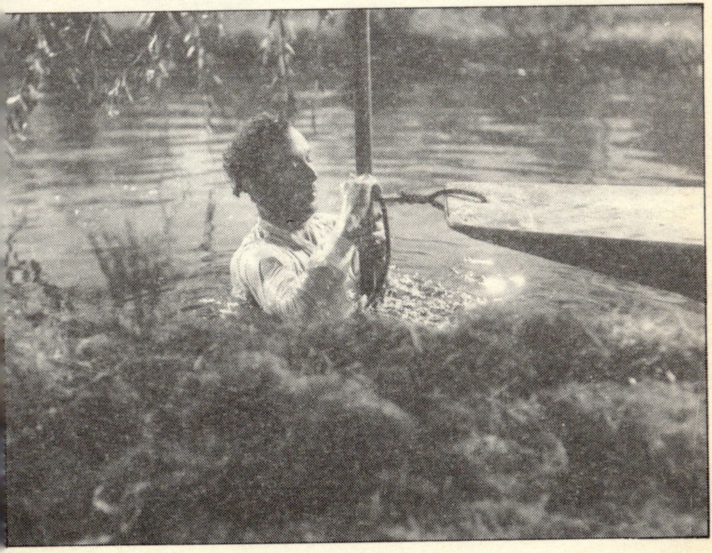

Next on the list is the unfortunate 24-year-old Henry D'Ascoyne whom Louis befriends through a common interest in photography. Louis spends a great deal of time on his estate getting to know him and his wife.

Louis arranges things so that one day Henry's amibitious photographic darkroom accidentally goes up in flames.

Agatha, in her attempts to further the cause of the suffragettes, advertises for votes for women from a balloon in Hyde Park.

DEVELOPER
FIXING SOLUTION

WOMEN of BRITAIN
FIGHT for Your
RIGHTS

Louis takes full advantage of this and from his third-floor rooms in Park Lane he shoots an arrow in the air, thereby puncturing her Ladyship's latest invention.

Finally, Louis turns to Lord Ascoyne D'Ascoyne, who is a banker for whom Louis works. Conveniently and mysteriously, the lord has a stroke (a result of Louis's poison), thereby leading Louis to the title of Louis D'Ascoyne Mazzini, 10th Duke of Chalfont.

Unfortunately, Louis, having made the title his, is finally suspected of murder and is tried for murder by his peers in the House of Lords.

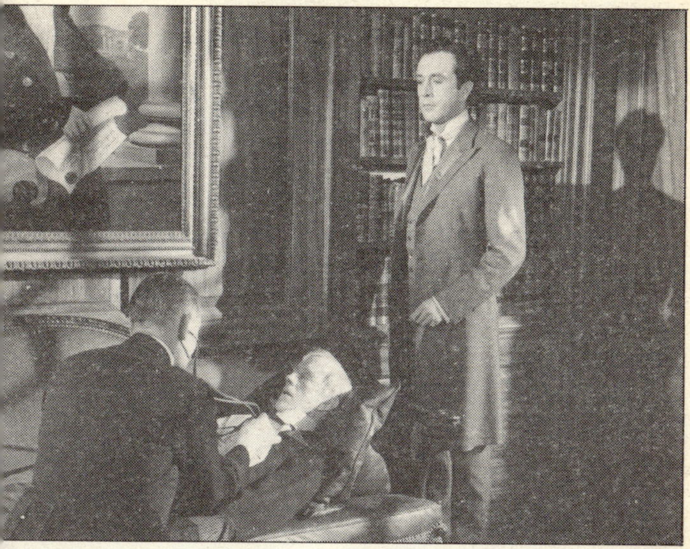

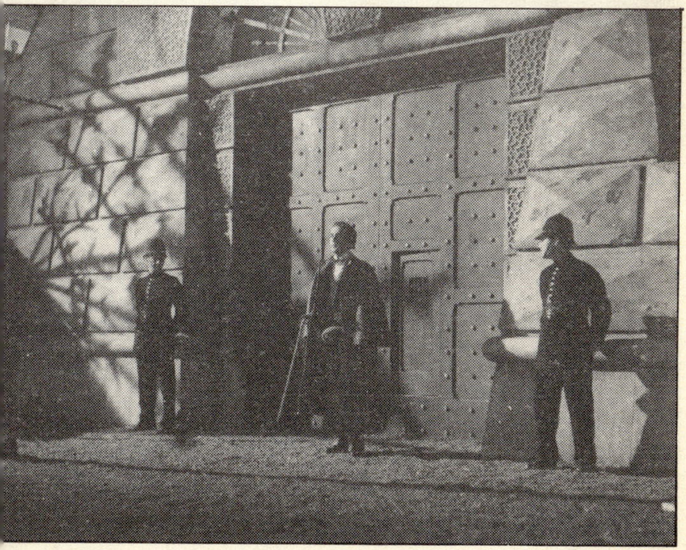

What you saw

1. What was the name of the ale and the stout being sold at the pub you first saw? ☐

2. How many locals were sitting or standing outside the pub? ☐

3. How many chimney pots were seen on Henry D'Ascoyne's mansion? ☐

4. Louis is seen outside the prison . . . what is he holding in his right hand? ☐

5. Lady Agatha's balloon had a sign on the front of it. What was the first line? ☐

What you read

1. What was Louis's mother's father's title? ☐

2. When did Louis's father die? ☐

3. How did Louis dispose of Henry D'Ascoyne? ☐

4. Where does Louis's second victim die? ☐

5. What floor was Louis's apartment in Park Lane? ☐

TOTAL SCORE ☐

TEST 5: GENERAL KNOWLEDGE

Important: read Introduction on page 15 first.
This test should be completed in 5 minutes.
Score 1 point for each correct answer.

1. Who was Henry VIII's second wife, and mother of Elizabeth I?

2. Who wrote the novels *The Bell* and *A Severed Head*?

3. Only one British prime minister was murdered whilst in office; who was he?

4. In which sport are competitions held for the Pershing Trophy and the Queen's Prize at Bisley?

5. Who wrote the music for the ballets 'The Fire Bird' and 'The Rite of Spring'?

6. Which organ of the body would be affected by strabismus or retinitis?

7. In poetry, how many syllables are there in a line called an iambic pentameter?

8. What name is given to a distance of 1/10 of a nautical mile?

9. Fortran, Cobol and Algol are all names of what?

10. Of which language is Walloon a dialect, spoken mainly in Belgium?

11. Which famous Frenchman is buried at Colombey Les Deux Eglises?

12. Which silent film comedian starred in 'The General', 'Steamboat Bill Junior' and 'The Navigator'?

13. Crossed golden keys are the emblem of which saint?

14. For which film did Peter Finch win a posthumous Oscar in 1976 as a deranged news reader?

15. What network did the astronomer Schiaparelli discover by telescope in 1877?

16. The Kiel Canal connects the North Sea with which other sea?

17. Which colour of ball in snooker scores 3 points?

18. The Royal Greenwich Observatory is now based at which castle in Sussex?

19. Montezuma was emperor of which nation in the 16th century in Mexico?

20. Who wrote the early detective novels *The Moonstone* and *The Woman in White*?

TOTAL SCORE

Answers

PROGRAMME 1
TEST 2: MENTAL AGILITY

1. **KRYPTON**.

2. PUZZLES. A = Z
B = Y
C = X   etc.

3. Yes – see below.

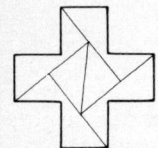

4. He is Percy's great grandson.

5. From left-hand corner: 1 7 6 3 4 8 2 9 5.

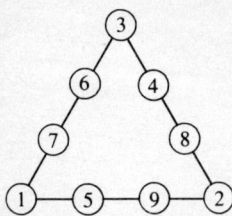

6. th (1st 2nd 3rd 4th 5th).

7. V.

8.   6 15 16
12 24 28
(1st column multiplied by 2
2nd column multiplied by 3
3rd column multiplied by 4)

9. Yes.

10. The sixth floor.

PROGRAMME 1
TEST 3: INTELLIGENCE

1. 128.

2. AB = 4 inches.

3. Follow these moves:
   - – – BW BW **BW BW**
   - WB BW **BW** B – – W
   - **WB BW** – – BBWW
   - W – WBBBBWW
   - WWWW BBBB –

4. A problem for an answer: arrange the missing numbers
   1 – 10 inclusive and 27 – 36 inclusive so that the sum of
   each column and row is 111. Now it's easy!

5. a) 1st Fred, 2nd Joe, 3rd Shaun, 4th Mick, 5th Bert.
   b) 1st French, 2nd Irish, 3rd English, 4th Japanese,
      5th American.
   c) Coffee.

PROGRAMME 1
TEST 4: OBSERVATION

What you saw

1. Glasses.
2. 2 large stars.
3. A sweater.
4. The navigation table.
5. 5, including the
   helicopter pad.

What you read

1. 6½ weeks.
2. 25 per cent of NATO's
   individual oil purchases.
3. A 30-foot statue of a god.
4. *The Flying Saucer.*
5. In Washington DC.

PROGRAMME 1
TEST 5: GENERAL KNOWLEDGE

1. Every 5 years.
2. Arnold Bennett.
3. Brandy.
4. 'The Godfather'.
5. Jupiter or Jove.
6. Turin.
7. William the Conqueror or William I.
8. Ireland.
9. North Channel.
10. Jersey.
11. Cycling.
12. Chewing gum.
13. The Marx Brothers.
14. Samuel Langhorne Clemens.
15. 1945.
16. Bonnie Prince Charlie or Charles Edward Stuart.
17. Faye Dunaway.
18. Cake.
19. Ku Klux Klan.
20. 1500 metres.

PROGRAMME 2
TEST 2: MENTAL AGILITY

1. S.   (Monday, Tuesday, Wednesday etc.)

2.

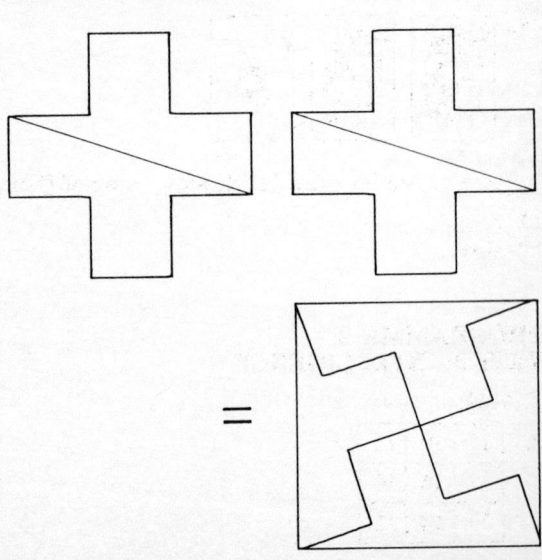

3. Cypher.

Capital letters stand for the letter before them:

e.g.   D = C
       Z = Y
       F = E

Lower case letters stand for the letter after them:

e.g.   o = P
       g = H
       q = R

4. No.

5. M.

6. 5.   (20 + 1 ÷ 7 = 3
         14 + 4 ÷ 6 = 3
          8 + 7 ÷ 3 = 5)

7. 50.   (Coins in sequence.)

8. 1944.   (18 × 108.)

9.

Ace of Spades   King of Spades   King of Diamonds.

10. 5.
    Rise.

PROGRAMME 2
TEST 3: INTELLIGENCE

1. 1019.

2.

17	10	15
12	14	16
13	18	11

3. If you persisted, you did it!

4.

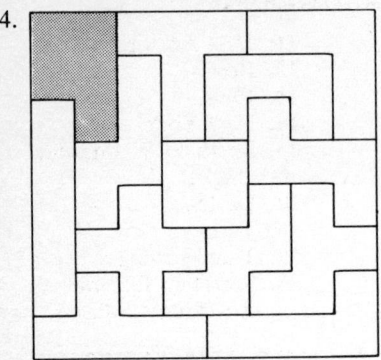

5. Split the balls into 3 groups of 4. Weigh 2 of the groups (first). If they balance then heavy ball is in third group. Take 2 balls from third group and weigh against 2 from another group (second). If they balance then heavy ball is in remaining 2. Weigh remaining 2 to discover heavy ball (third).

If the 2 groups do not balance on first weighing then you know in which group the heavy ball is – follow deductive course similar to one outlined above.

PROGRAMME 2
TEST 4: OBSERVATION

What you saw

1. 2.
2. 2.
3. A banana skin.
4. Coconut shells.
5. Bagheera's.

What you read

1. 10 years old.
2. In the direction of the setting sun – the west.
3. The secret of the red flower . . . fire.
4. The Dawn Patrol.
5. The Black Swamp, the trees of snakes and the ruined city.

PROGRAMME 2
TEST 5: GENERAL KNOWLEDGE

1. Cairo.
2. Bat.
3. Fidel Castro.
4. St Leger.
5. Excalibur.
6. 'The Tempest'.
7. Yachting or sailing.
8. William IV.
9. Trapezium.
10. Regent Street.
11. Jane Austen.
12. Bones.
13. Elba.
14. New York.
15. Sheffield Wednesday.
16. Cricket.
17. Derby.
18. Turkey.
19. Thanksgiving.
20. Secretary General of the United Nations.

PROGRAMME 3
TEST 2: MENTAL AGILITY

1. 10, J.   (Cards 1 to 10, Jack, Queen, King and Ace.)

2.

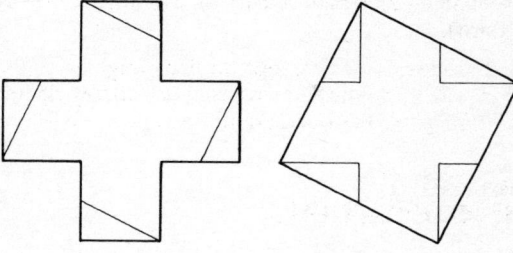

3. Resolve.

   A = 1
   B = 2   etc.

   Word is simply reversed i.e.   E = 5
                                   V = 22
                                   L = 12
                                   O = 15 etc.

4. No.

5. J.

6.

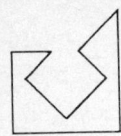

(Rotate 90° anticlockwise & draw mirror image.)

7. 1.45.　　(Clock times at 11- 22- 33- 44-minute intervals.)

8. u.　　(Interval between letters increases by one each time i.e. a-c--f---j and capitals and lower-case alternate.)

9. Alternating top and bottom halves of A B C D E F etc.

10. John is Otto's great grandson.

PROGRAME 3
TEST 3: INTELLIGENCE

1. 294 miles.

2.

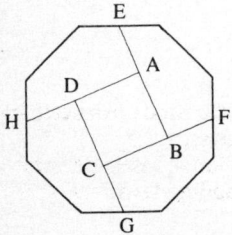

a) Sides of square = sides of octagon.
b) Draw through AD, DC, CB and BA until line hits octagon side – at points E, F, G and H. These points *should* be in the middle of their side.
c) The angles EAD, HDC, GCB and FBA are right-angled.

3. 15 moves in all, as follows:

Move	white	1
2	blacks	3
3	whites	6
3	blacks	9
3	whites	12
2	blacks	14
1	white	15 moves

4.

3	71	5	23
53	**11**	37	1
17	13	**41**	31
28	7	18	**47**

5.   9 5 6 7
     1 0 8 5
     _____
     1 0 6 5 2

PROGRAMME 3
TEST 4: OBSERVATION

What you saw

1. Nothing.
2. 5.
3. 3.
4. A horse.
5. A spear.

What you read

1. Its twin suns.
2. The white castle.
3. 7.
4. The sands from her hourglass.
5. Plunge his hand into boiling lava.

PROGRAMME 3
TEST 5: GENERAL KNOWLEDGE

1. Harold Wilson.
2. 'Jocky' Wilson.
3. J. M. Synge.
4. Edvard Grieg.
5. Dog.
6. Rowing or sculling, on the Thames.
7. Sturgeon.
8. Christiaan Barnard.
9. Owl.
10. Frank Richards.
11. Mel Brooks.
12. Tees.
13. Tourist Trophy.
14. The Gillette Cup.
15. 4.
16. Delta.
17. Southampton.
18. Colombia.
19. Dove or pigeon.
20. Raven.

PROGRAMME 4
TEST 2: MENTAL AGILITY

1. 18.   (Clockwise round dartboard.)

2.

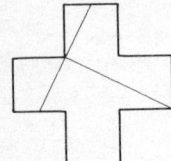 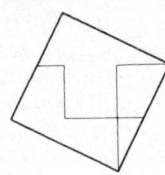

3. 'Must'.   (M is 13th letter of alphabet – reverse to 31, U is 21st letter of alphabet – reverse to 12, etc.)

4. Yes.

5. 17.

6. 12 1 4 5.   (Opposite numbers on a clock face i.e., 6 is opposite to 12, 3 is opposite 9, etc.)

7. 1.   (Square roots of 5 4 3 2 1 respectively.)

8. E.   (January, February, March, etc.)

9. 3.

10. Pick up No. 2 and pour into No. 5.

PROGRAMME 4
TEST 3: INTELLIGENCE

1. There are only 9 possible differences, each of which is a multiple of 99. $7 \times 99 = 693$, and this is the only one which ends in 3.

2. 40 feet.

3. 9.

4.

4	6	6	3
4	4	5	6
5	5	5	4
6	4	3	6

5. a Work out all the likely products i.e. $6 \times 4 \times 3$.
   b Add up each group of 3. 2 of the groups add up to the same number (i.e. "There's not enough information.").
   c Which of the 2 groups has a unique larger number? (His eldest daughter plays the violin.)

   You now have their ages: 8, 3 and 3.

PROGRAMME 4
TEST 4: OBSERVATION

What you saw

1. A dolphin leaping in a circle.
2. A whistle on a string.
3. A metal triangle.
4. 5.
5. 4.40 approximately.

What you read

1. South America.
2. A scenic marvel of make-believe coral reefs.
3. In a hillside pavilion.
4. With the Scripps Marine Institute.
5. Kelly Ann Bukowski.

PROGRAMME 4
TEST 5: GENERAL KNOWLEDGE

1. Glenn Miller.
2. Fish.
3. Benjamin Britten.
4. Glasgow Celtic.
5. Charles Darwin.
6. Tanzania.
7. A clay oven.
8. Marie Antoinette.
9. Jane Eyre.
10. River Plate.
11. Baseball.
12. Orkney.
13. Euphonium.
14. Ipswich Town.
15. 'On Golden Pond'.
16. Ag.
17. Motor cycling.
18. Richard Wagner.
19. Smallpox.
20. Louisa May Alcott.

PROGRAMME 5
TEST 2: MENTAL AGILITY

1. V. (Red, Orange, Yellow, Green, Blue, Indigo, Violet – Newton's colours of the spectrum.)

2.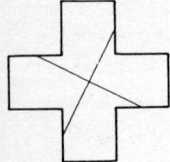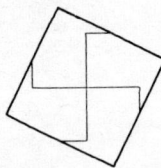

3. Problems. (P = Q
   R = S T
   O = P Q R
   B = C
   L = M N
   E = F G H   etc.)

4. No.

5. 21.

6.

(Rotate image through 90° clockwise. Draw mirror image colouring light areas dark and leaving dark areas white.)

7. 1500. (Wavelengths in metres of ratios, 1, 2, 3 and 4.)

8. 21.50. (24-hour clock going backwards in 2 hrs 17 mins jumps.)

9. Tents. (Hour hand. Initial letters of the hour indicated. Twelve, Eleven, Nine, Ten, Six.)

10. 4 weights:1, 3, 9 and 27.   1 oz = DIAGRAM
                                2 oz = DIAGRAM
                                3 oz = DIAGRAM
                                4 oz = DIAGRAM
                                5 oz = DIAGRAM
                                6 oz = DIAGRAM

PROGRAMME 5
TEST 3: INTELLIGENCE

1. $\dfrac{1419}{846 \ \sqrt{1200474}}$

2.

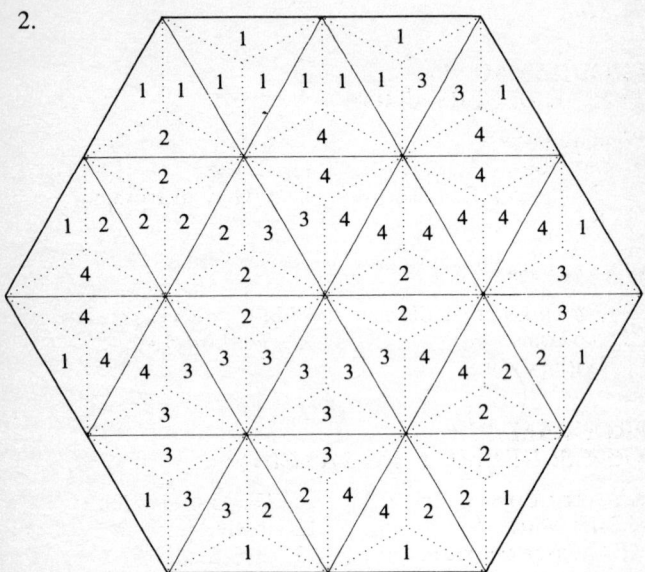

3. R pushes P into A.
   R returns and pushes Q up to P in A.
   R couples Q to P and pulls both out to F.
   R pushes them to E.
   P is uncoupled.
   R takes Q back to A and leaves it there.
   R returns to P, takes P to C and leaves it there.
   R running successively through FDB, comes to A, pulls
     Q out and leaves it at B.

4. 10   2
   11   6
    9   4
     13   5

5. 64.

PROGRAMME 5
TEST 4: OBSERVATION

What you saw
1. Fremlins.
2. 3.
3. 8.

4. A cane.
5. Women in Britain.

What you read
1. 7th Duke of Chalfont.
2. At Louis's birth.
3. With poison.

4. In his own darkroom.
5. The third floor.

PROGRAMME 5
TEST 5: GENERAL KNOWLEDGE

1. Anne Boleyn.
2. Iris Murdoch.
3. Spencer Perceval.
4. Shooting of Rifles.
5. Stravinsky.
6. The eye.
7. Ten.
8. Cable.
9. Computer Languages.
10. French.

11. General De Gaulle.
12. Buster Keaton.
13. St Peter.
14. Network.
15. Canals on Mars – which probably don't exist.
16. Baltic.
17. Green.
18. Herstmonceux.
19. Aztecs.
20. Wilkie Collins.

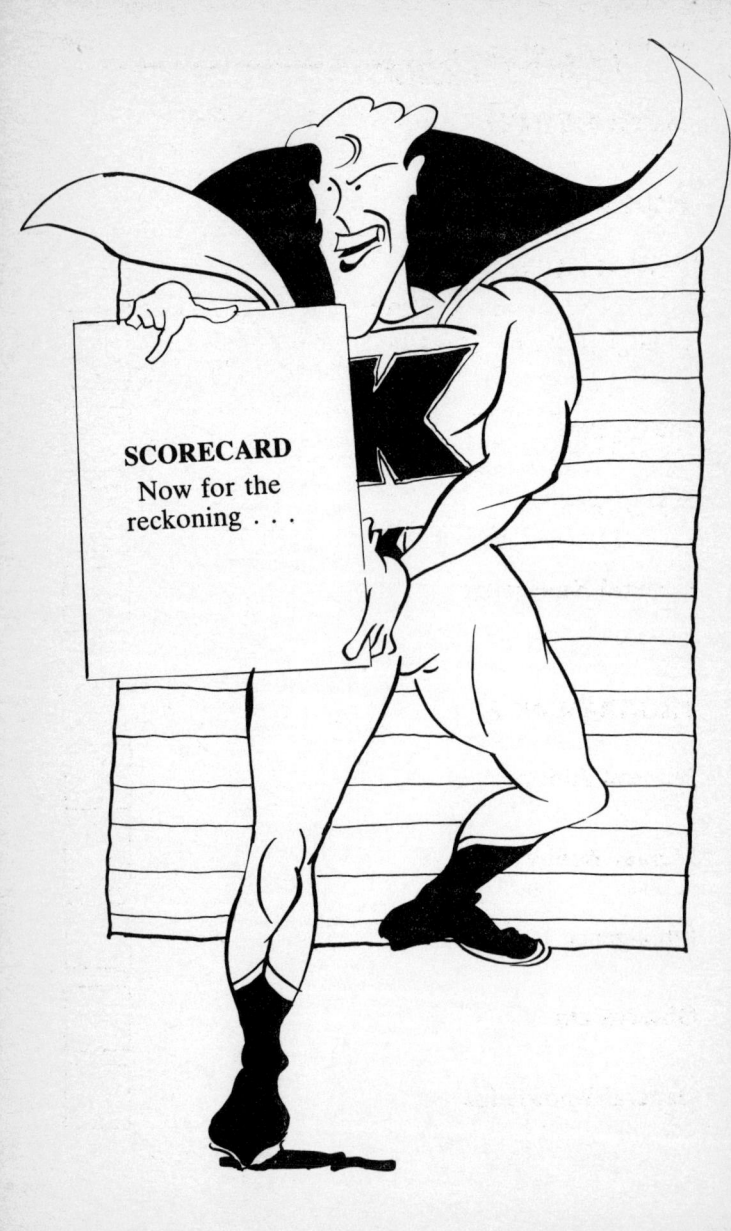

Scorecard

PROGRAMME 1

Physical Ability

Mental Agility

Intelligence

Observation

General Knowledge

PROGRAMME 2

Physical Ability

Mental Agility

Intelligence

Observation

General Knowledge

Scorecard

PROGRAMME 3

Physical Ability

Mental Agility

Intelligence

Observation

General Knowledge

PROGRAMME 4

Physical Ability

Mental Agility

Intelligence

Observation

General Knowledge

Scorecard

PROGRAMME 5

Physical Ability

Mental Agility

Intelligence

Observation

General Knowledge

—The Krypton Factor—
APPLICATION FORM

NAME: _____

AGE: _____ SEX: _____

DATE OF BIRTH: _____

MARITAL STATUS: _____

OCCUPATION: _____

ADDRESS: _____

_____

_____

WORK TELEPHONE NO: _____

HOME TELEPHONE NO: _____

MESSAGE CAN BE LEFT WITH TELEPHONE NO: _____

HEIGHT: _____ WEIGHT: _____

SPORTS PLAYED: _____

_____

_____

ANY OTHER INTERESTS: _____

_____

_____

Please turn over and complete scores.

──The Krypton Factor──

MY KRYPTON FACTOR SCORES IN EACH TEST WERE:

Programmes:	1	2	3	4	5
Mental Agility					
Physical Ability					
Intelligence					
Observation					
General Knowledge					

Past Winners

Previous winners of 'The Krypton Factor' were:

1977 Harry Evans
1978 Ken Wilmshurst
1979 Peter Richardson
1980 Philip Bradley
1981 John McAllister
1982 John Webley
1983 Chris Topham

BESTSELLING NON-FICTION FROM ARROW

All these books are available from your bookshop or newsagent or you can order them direct. Just tick the titles you want and complete the form below.

☐	THE GREAT ESCAPE	Paul Brickhill	£1.60
☐	A RUMOR OF WAR	Philip Caputo	£1.95
☐	SS WEREWOLF	Charles Whiting	£1.50
☐	A LITTLE ZIT ON THE SIDE	Jasper Carrott	£1.25
☐	THE ART OF COARSE ACTING	Michael Green	£1.50
☐	THE UNLUCKIEST MAN IN THE WORLD	Mike Harding	£1.50
☐	DIARY OF A SOMEBODY	Christopher Matthew	£1.25
☐	TALES FROM A LONG ROOM	Peter Tinniswood	£1.75
☐	LOVE WITHOUT FEAR	Eustace Chesser	£1.95
☐	NO CHANGE	Wendy Cooper	£1.75
☐	MEN IN LOVE	Nancy Friday	£2.50

Postage _____

Total _____

ARROW BOOKS, BOOKSERVICE BY POST, PO BOX 29, DOUGLAS, ISLE OF MAN, BRITISH ISLES

Please enclose a cheque or postal order made out to Arrow Books Ltd for the amount due including 15p per book for postage and packing both for orders within the UK and for overseas orders.

Please print clearly

NAME ....

ADDRESS ....

....

Whilst every effort is made to keep prices down and to keep popular books in print, Arrow Books cannot guarantee that prices will be the same as those advertised here or that the books will be available.

TEST YOUR OWN SUPERMIND

Your hidden powers and how to use them

David Adams

Telepathy, ESP, telekinesis, precognition, psychic healing —
are they paranormal powers possessed by the fortunate few —
or mental skills which are latent in all of us?

In this astonishing book psychologist David Adams presents
the evidence that has convinced even the most sceptical
scientists that such powers exist — and shows how you can
unlock the secrets of your own supermind and use the powers
that lie dormant within you.

TEST YOUR OWN SUPERMIND is based on detailed case
histories, reports of investigations and scientific research into
every aspect of the paranormal: and contains exercises that
enable you to tap your hidden powers and put them to work.